André John

Proceedings of a board of general officers respecting Major

John André

André John

Proceedings of a board of general officers respecting Major John André

ISBN/EAN: 9783337727420

Printed in Europe, USA, Canada, Australia, Japan

Cover: Foto ©ninafisch / pixelio.de

More available books at **www.hansebooks.com**

PROCEEDINGS

OF A

BOARD

OF

GENERAL OFFICERS,

HELD BY ORDER OF

His Excellency Gen. WASHINGTON,

Commander in Chief of the Army of the United States
of AMERICA.

RESPECTING

Major *JOHN ANDRÉ*,

Adjutant General of the Britiſh Army.

SEPTEMBER 29, 1780.

PHILADELPHIA:
Printed by FRANCIS BAILEY, in Market-Street
M.DCC.LXXX.

EXTRACTS of LETTERS

from General WASHINGTON, *to the* PRESIDENT *of* CONGRESS.

Robifon's Houfe, in the Highlands, Sept. 26, 1780.

S I R,

I HAVE the honor to inform Congrefs, that I arrived here yefterday about twelve o'clock, on my return from Hartford. Some hours previous to my arrival Major General Arnold went from his quarters, which were this place, and, as it was fuppofed, over the river to the garrifon at Weft Point, whither I proceeded myfelf, in order to vifit the poft. I found General Arnold had not been there during the day, and on my return to his quarters he was ftill abfent. In the mean time, a packet had arrived from Lieut. Colonel Jamefon, announcing the capture of a John Anderfon, who was endeavouring to go to New-York with feveral interefting and important papers, all in the hand writing of General Arnold. This was alfo accompanied with a letter from the prifoner, avowing himfelf to be Major John André, Adjutant General to the Britifh army, relating the manner of his capture, and endeavouring to fhew that he did not come under the defcription of a *fpy.* From thefe feveral circumftances, and information that the General feemed to be thrown into fome degree of agitation, on receiving a letter a little time before he went from his quarters, I was led to conclude immediately that he had heard of Major André's captivity, and that he would, if poffible, efcape to the enemy, and accordingly took fuch meafures as appeared the moft probable to apprehend him. But he had embarked in a barge and proceeded down the river, under a flag, to the Vulture

fhip

fhip of war, which lay at fome miles below Stoney and Verplank's Points. He wrote me a letter after he got on board. Major André is not arrived yet, but I hope he is fecure, and that he will be here to-day. I have been and am taking precautions, which I truft will prove effectual to prevent the important confequences which this conduct, on the part of General Arnold, was intended to produce. I do not know the party that took Major André, but it is faid that it confifted only of a few militia, who acted in fuch a manner upon the occafion, as does them the higheft honor, and proves them to be men of great virtue. As foon as I know their names, I fhall take pleafure in tranf-mitting them to Congrefs.

Paramus, October 7, 1780.

SIR,

I HAVE the honour to enclofe Congrefs a copy of the proceedings of a Board of General Officers in the cafe of Major André Adjutant General to the Britifh army. This officer was executed in purfuance of the opinion of the Board, on Monday, the 2d inftant, at 12 o'clock, at our late camp at Tappan. Befides the proceedings I tranfmit copies of fundry letters refpecting the matter, which are all that paffed on the fubject, not included in the proceedings.

I have now the pleafure to communicate the names of the three perfons who captured Major André, and who refufed to releafe him, notwithftanding the moft earneft importunities and affurances of a liberal reward on his part. Their names are, *John Paulding, David Williams,* and *Ifaac Van Wert.*

PROCEEDINGS

GEORGE THE THIRD.

P R O C E E D I N G S

O F A

Board of General Officers,

Held by Order of his Excellency General WASHINGTON,
commander in chief of the army of the United States
of America, refpecting Major André, Adjutant General
of the Britifh army, September the 29th, 1780, at
Tappan, in the State of New-York.

P R E S E N T,

Major General Greene, Prefident,
Major General Lord Stirling,
Major General St. Clair,
Major General The Marquis de la Fayette,
Major General Howe,
Major General The Baron de Steuben,
Brigadier General Parfons,
Brigadier General Clinton,
Brigadier General Knox,
Brigadier General Glover,
Brigadier General Patterfon,
Brigadier General Hand,
Brigadier General Huntington,
Brigadier General Starke,
John Lawrence, Judge-Advocate General.

MAJOR André, Adjutant General to the Britifh army
was brought before the Board, and the following
letter from General Wafhington, to the Board, dated
Head Quarters, Tappan, September 29th, 1780, was laid
before them and read.

" *Gentlemen,*
" Major André, Adjutant General to the Britifh army,
" will be brought before you for your examination. He
" came within our lines in the night, on an interview
" with Major General Arnold, and in an affumed charac-
" ter; and was taken within our lines, in a difguifed ha-
" bit, with a pafs under a feigned name, and with the
" inclofed papers concealed upon him. After a careful
" examination,

" examination, you will be pleafed, as fpeedily as poffi-
" ble, to report a precife ftate of his cafe, together with
" your opinion of the light in which he ought to be con-
" fidered, and the punishment that ought to be inflicted.
" The Judge Advocate will attend to affift in the exami-
" nation, who has fundry other papers relative to this
" matter, which he will lay before the Board.
   " *I have the honour to be,*
    " *Gentlemen,*
     " *Your moft obedient and humble fervant,*
      " G. WASHINGTON.
" *The Board of General Officers*
 convened at Tappan."

The names of the officers compofing the Board were
read to Major André, and on his being afked whether he
confeffed the matters contained in the letter from his Excellency General Wafhington to the Board, or denied them,
*he said, in addition to his letter to General Wafhington,
dated Salem, the 24th September,* 1780. (which was read
to the board, and acknowledged by Major André, to have
been written by him, which letter is as follows:

       Salem, 24th Sept. 1780.
 " S I R,
 " *What I have as yet faid concerning myfelf, was in the
" juftifiable attempt to be extricated; I am too little accuf-
" tomed to duplicity to have fucceeded.*
 " *I beg your Excellency will be perfuaded, that no alter-
" ation in the temper of my mind, or apprehenfion for my
" fafety, induces me to take the ftep of addreffing you, but
" that it is to fecure myfelf from an imputation of having
" affumed a mean character for treacherous purpofes or
" felf intereft. A conduct incompatible with the principles
" that actuated me, as well as with my condition in life.*
 " *It is to vindicate my fame that I fpeak and not to fo-
" licit fecurity.*
 " *The perfon in your poffeffion is Major John Andre,
" Adjutant General to the Britifh army.*
 " *The influence of one commander in the army of his
" adverfary is an advantage taken in war. A correfpon-
" dence for this purpofe I held; as confidential (in the pre-
" fent inftance) with his Excellency Sir Henry Clinton.*
 " *To favour it, I agreed to meet upon ground not
" within pofts of either army, a perfon who was to give
" me intelligence; I came up in the Vulture man of war*
            for

" *for this effect, and was fetched by a boat from the shore to*
" *the beach: Being there I was told that the approach of day*
" *would prevent my return, and that I must be concealed*
" *until the next night. I was in my regimentals and had*
" *fairly risked my person.*

" *Against my stipulation, my intention and without my*
" *knowledge before hand, I was conducted within one of*
" *your posts. Your Excellency may conceive` my sensation*
" *on this occasion and will imagine how much more I must*
" *have been affected, by a refusal to reconduct me back*
" *the next night as I had been brought. Thus become a*
" *prisoner I had to concert my escape.* I quitted my uni-
" *form and was passed another way in the night without*
" *the American posts to neutral ground, and informed I was*
" *beyond all armed parties `and left to press for New-York.*
" *I was taken at Tarry Town by some volunteers.*

" *Thus as I have had the honor to relate was I betrayed*
" *(being Adjutant General of the British army) into the*
" *vile condition of an enemy in disguise within your posts.*

" *Having avowed myself a British officer I have nothing*
" *to reveal but what relates to myself, which is true on*
" *the honour of an officer and a gentleman.*

" *The request I have to make your Excellency, and I am*
" *conscious I address myself well, is, that in any rigour*
" *policy may dictate, a decency of conduct towards me may*
" *mark, that though unfortunate I am branded with no-*
" *thing dishonourable, as no motive could be mine but the*
" *service of my king, and as I was involuntarily an impostor.*

" *Another request is, that I may be permitted to write*
" *an open letter to Sir Henry Clinton and another to a*
" *friend for cloaths and linen.*

" *I take the liberty to mention the condition of some*
" *gentlemen at Charles-Town, who being either on parole*
" *or under protection, were engaged in a conspiracy against*
" *us. Though their situation is not similar, they are objects*
" *who may be set in exchange for me, or are persons whom*
" *the treatment I receive might affect.*

" *It is no less, Sir, in a confidence in the generosity of your*
" *mind, than on account of your superior station that I have*
" *chosen to importune you with this letter.*

" *I have the honour to be, with great respect, Sir,*
" *Your Excellency's most obedient*
" *and most humble servant,*
" *JOHN ANDRE,*
" *Adjutant General.*"

His Excellency General Washington.
&c. &c &c.)   That

That he came on fhore from the Vulture floop of war in *the night* of the twenty-firft of September inftant, fomewhere under the Haverftraw mountain; that the boat he came on fhore in carried *no flag*, and that he had on a furtout coat over his regimentals, and that he wore his furtout coat when he was taken; that he met General Arnold on the fhore, and had an interview with him there. He alfo faid, that when he left the Vulture floop of war, it was underftood he was to return that night; but it was then doubted, and if he could not return he was promifed to be *concealed on* fhore in a place of fafety, until the next *night*, when he was to return in the fame manner he came on fhore; and when the next day came he was folicitous to get back, and made enquiries in the courfe of the day, how he fhould return, when he was informed he could not return that way and he muft take the rout he did afterwards. He alfo faid, That the firft notice he had of his being within any *of our pofts*, was, being challenged by the fentry, which was the firft night he was on fhore. He alfo faid, that the evening of the twenty-fecond of September inftant, he paffed *King's Ferry between our pofts of Stoney and Verplank's Points*, in the *drefs he is at prefent in, and which he faid was not his regimentals*, and which drefs he procured, after he landed from the Vulture and when he was within *our pofts*, and that he was proceeding to New-York, but was taken on his way at Tarry Town, as he has mentioned in his letter, on Saturday the twenty-third of September inftant, about nine o'clock in the morning.

The following papers were laid before the Board and fhewn to Major André, who confeffed to the board that they were found on him when he was taken, and faid they were concealed in his boot, except the pafs:-----

A pafs from General Arnold to *John Anderson*, which name Major André *acknowledged he affumed.*

Artillery orders, September 5, 1780.

Eftimate of the force at Weft Point and its dependencies, September 1780.

Eftimate of men to man the works at Weft Point, &c.

Return of ordnance at Weft Point, September 1780.

Remarks on works at Weft Point.

Copy of a ftate of matters laid before a council of war, by his Excellency General Wafhington, held the 6th of September 1780.

A letter

GEN. LORD STIRLING

A letter figned *John Anderfon*, dated Sept. 7, 1780, to Colonel Sheldon *, was alfo laid before the Board, and fhewn to Major Andrè, which *he acknowledged* to have been written by *him*, and is as follows :

" S I R,   " *New-York, the 7th Sept.* 1780.

" I AM told *my name* is made known to you, and that " I may hope your indulgence in permitting me to meet " a friend near your out pofts. *I* will endeavour to ob-" tain permiffion to go out *with a flag* which will be fent " to Dobb's Ferry on Monday next, the 11th, at twelve " o'clock, when I fhall be happy to meet Mr. G--- §.

" Should I not be allowed to go, the officer who is to " command the efcort, between whom and myfelf no " diftinction need be made, can fpeak on the affair.

" Let me entreat you, Sir, to favour a matter fo in-" terefting to the parties concerned, and which is of fo " private a nature that the public on neither fide can be " injured by it.

" I fhall be happy on my part in doing any act of kind-" nefs to you in a family or property concern of a fimilar " nature.

" I truft I fhall not be detained, but fhould any old " grudge be a caufe for it, I fhall rather rifk that, than " neglect the bufinefs in queftion, *or affume a myfterious* " *character* to carry on an innocent affair, and, as friends " have advifed, get· to your lines by ftealth. I am, Sir, " with all regard,

" *Your moft obedient humble fervant,*

. " JOHN ANDERSON."

" *Col.* SHELDON."

---

* *Left it fhould be fuppofed that Colonel Sheldon, to whom the above letter is addreffed, was privy to the plot carrying on by general Arnold, it is to be obferved, that the letter was found among Arnold's papers, and had been tranfmitted by Colonel Sheldon, who, it appears from a letter of the 9th of September to Arnold, which inclofed it, had never heard of John Anderfon before. Arnold in his anfwer on the 10th, acknowledged he had not communicated it to him, though he had informed him that he expected a perfon would come from New-York, for the purpofe of bringing him intelligence.*

(§) *It appears by the fame letter that Arnold had written to Mr. Anderfon, under the fignature of Guftavus. His words are " I was obliged to write with great caution to him, my letter was figned Guftavus to prevent any difcovery in cafe it fell into the hands of the enemy."*

B

Major André obferved that this letter could be of no force in the cafe in queftion, as it was written in New-York, when he was under the orders of General Clinton, but that it tended to prove that it was not his intention to come within our lines.

The Board having interrogated Major André about his conception of his coming on fhore under the fanction of a flag, *he faid, That it was impoffible for him to fuppofe he came on fhore under that fanction*; and added, That if he came on fhore under that fanction, he certainly might have returned under it.

Major André having acknowledged the preceding facts, and being afked whether he had any thing to fay refpecting them, anfwered, He left them to operate with the Board.

The examination of Major André being concluded, he was remanded into cuftody.

The following letters were laid before the Board, and read:——Benedict Arnold's letter to General Wafhington, dated September 25, 1780. Col. Robinfon's letter to General Wafhington, dated September 25, 1780, and general Clinton's letter, dated the 26th September, 1780, (inclofing a letter of the fame date from Benedict Arnold) to General Wafhington.

" *On board the Vulture, Sept.* 25, 1780.

" S I R,

" T H E heart which is confcious of its own rectitude, cannot attempt to palliate a ftep which the world may cenfure as wrong; I have ever acted from a principle of love to my country, fince the commencement of the prefent unhappy conteft between Great-Britain and the Colonies; the fame principle of love to my country actuates my prefent conduct, however it may appear inconfiftent to the world, who very feldom judge right of any man's actions.

" I have no favour to afk for myfelf. I have too often experienced the ingratitude of my country to attempt it; but from the known humanity of your Excellency, I am induced to afk your protection for Mrs. Arnold, from every infult and injury that the miftaken vengeance of my country may expofe her to. It ought to fall only on me; fhe is as good and as innocent as an angel, and is incapable of doing wrong. I beg fhe may be permitted to return to her friends in Philadelphia, or to come to me as fhe may choofe; from your Excellency I have no fears

on

on her account, but fhe may fuffer from the miftaken fury of the country.

" I have to requeft that the inclofed letter may be delivered to Mrs. Arnold, and fhe permitted to write to me.

" I have alfo to afk that my cloaths and baggage, which are of little confequence, may be fent to me, if required their value fhall be paid in money.

" *I have the honour to be, with great regard and efteem,*
" *Your Excellency's moft obedient humble fervant,*
" B. ARNOLD."
His Excellency General Wafhington."

" N. B. In juftice to the gentlemen of my family, Col. Varrick and Major Franks, I think myfelf in honour bound to declare, that they, as well as Jofhua Smith, Efq; (who I know is fufpefted) are totally ignorant of any tranfaftions of mine, that they had reafon to believe were injurious to the public."

" *Vulture, off Sinfinck, Sept.* 25, 1780.

" *S I R,*

" I A M this moment informed that Major Andrè, Adjutant General of his Majefty's army in America, is detained as a prifoner, by the army under your command. It is therefore incumbent on me to inform you of the manner of his falling into your hands : He went up with a flag at the requeft of General Arnold, on public bufinefs with him, and had his permit to return by land to New-York : Under thefe circumftances Major Andrè cannot be detained by you, without the greateft violation of flags, and contrary to the cuftom and ufage of all nations; and as I imagine you will fee this matter in the fame point of view as I do, I muft defire you will order him to be fet at liberty and allowed to return immediately : Every ftep Major Andrè took was by the advice and direftion of General Arnold, even that of taking a feigned name, and of courfe not liable to cenfure for it.

" *I am, Sir, not forgetting our former acquaintance,*
" *Your very humble fervant,*
" BEV. ROBINSON, Col.
Loyl. Americ."

" *His Excellency*
General WASHINGTON."

" *New-*

"*New-York, Sept.* 26, 1780.

" S I R,

" BEING informed that the King's Adjutant General in America has been ſtopt, under Major General Arnold's paſſports, and is detained a priſoner in your Excellency's army, I have the honour to inform you, Sir, that I permitted Major Andrè to go to Major General Arnold, at the particular requeſt of that general officer. You will perceive, Sir, by the incloſed paper, that a flag of truce was ſent to receive Major Andrè, and paſſports granted for his return, I therefore can have no doubt but your Excellency will immediately direct, that this officer has permiſſion to return to my orders at New-York.

" *I have the honour to be, your Excellency's*
" *moſt obedient and moſt humble ſervt.*
" H. CLINTON."

" *His Excellency General* WASHINGTON."

"*New-York, Sept.* 26, 1780.

" S I R,

" IN anſwer to your Excellency's meſſage, reſpecting your Adjutant General, Major Andrè, and deſiring my idea of the reaſons why he is detained, being under my paſſports, I have the honour to inform you, Sir, that I apprehend a few hours muſt return Major Andrè to your Excellency's orders, as that officer is aſſuredly under the protection of a flag of truce ſent by me to him for the purpoſe of a converſation which I requeſted to hold with him relating to myſelf, and which I wiſhed to communicate through that officer to your Excellency.

" I commanded at the time at Weſt Point, had an undoubted right to ſend my flag of truce for Major Andrè, who came to me under that protection, and having held my converſation with him, I delivered him confidential papers in my own hand writing, to deliver to your Excellency, thinking it much properer he ſhould return by land, I directed him to make uſe of the feigned name of John Anderſon, under which he had by my direction or come on ſhore, and gave him my paſſports to go to the White Plains on his way to New-York. This officer cannot therefore fail of being immediately ſent to New-York, as he was invited to a converſation with me, for which I ſent him a flag of truce, and finally gave him paſſports for his ſafe return to your Excellency ; all which I had then a right to do, being in the actual ſervice of America, under the orders of General

ral Wafhington, and commanding general at Weft Point and its dependencies.

" *I have the honour to be, your Excellency's*
   " *moft obedient and very humble fervant,*
                     " B. A R N O L D."
" *His Excellency Sir* HENRY CLINTON."

The Board having confidered the letter from his Excellency General Wafhington refpecting Major Andrè, Adjutant General to the Britifh army, the confeffion of Major Andrè, and the papers produced to them, REPORT
to His Excellency, the Commander in Chief, the following facts, which appear to them relative to Major Andrè.

Firft, That he came on fhore from the Vulture floop
of war in the *night* of the twenty-firft of September inftant, on an interview with General Arnold, *in a private
and fecret manner.*

Secondly, That *he changed his drefs within our lines, and
under a feigned name, and in a disguifed habit,* paffed our
works at Stoney and Verplank's Points, the evening of the
twenty-fecond of September inftant, and was taken the
morning of the twenty-third of September inftant, *at
Tarry Town, in a difguifed habit,* being then on his way
to New-York, *and when taken,* he had in his poffeffion
feveral papers, which contained *intelligence for the enemy.*

The Board having maturely confidered thefe facts, DO
ALSO REPORT to His Excellency General Wafhington, That Major Andrè, Adjutant General to the Britifh
army, ought to be confidered as a Spy from the enemy,
and that agreeable to the law and ufage of nations, it is
their opinion, he ought to fuffer death.

> NATH. GREENE, *M. Genl.* Prefident.
> *Stirling, M. G.*
> *Ar. St. Clair, M. G.*
> *La Fayette, M. G.*
> *R. Howe, M. G.*
> *Stuben, M. G.*
> *Saml. H. Parfons, B. Genl.*
> *James Clinton, B. Genl.*
> *H. Knox, Brigr. Genl. Artillery.*
> *Jno. Glover, B. Genl.*
> *John Patterfon, B. Genl.*
> *Edwd. Hand, B. Genl.*
> *J. Huntington, B. Genl.*
> *John Starke, B. Genl.*

> JOHN LAWRENCE, *J. A. Genl.*

APPENDIX.

Copy of a Letter from Major André, Adjutant General, to Sir Henry Clinton, K. B. &c. &c.

Tappan, Sept. 29, 1780.

SIR,

YOUR Excellency is doubtlefs already apprifed of the manner in which I was taken, and poffibly of the ferious light in which my conduct is confidered, and the rigorous determination that is impending.

Under thefe circumftances, I have obtained General Wafhington's permiffion to fend you this letter; the object of which is, to remove from your breaft any fuf-picion, that I could imagine I was bound by your Excellency's orders to expofe myfelf to what has happened. The events of coming within an enemy's pofts, and of changing my drefs, which led me to my prefent fituati-on, were contrary to my own intentions, as they were to your orders; and the circuitous route, which I took to return, was impofed (perhaps unavoidably) without alternative upon me.

I am perfectly tranquil in mind, and prepared for any fate, to which an honeft zeal for my King's fervice may have devoted me.

In addreffing myfelf to your Excellency on this occa-fion, the force of all my obligations to you, and of the attachment and gratitude I bear you, recurs to me. With all the warmth of my heart, I give you thanks for your Excellency's profufe kindnefs to me; and I fend you the moft earneft wifhes for your welfare, which a faith-ful, affectionate, and refpectful attendant can frame.

I have a mother and three fifters, to whom the value of my commiffion would be an object, as the lofs of Grenada has much affected their income. It is needlefs to be more explicit on this fubject; I am perfuaded of your Excellency's goodnefs.

I receive

.

I receive the greateſt attention from his Excellency General Waſhington, and from every perſon, under whoſe charge I happen to be placed.

I have the honour to be,
With the moſt reſpectful attachment,
Your Excellency's moſt obedient
and moſt humble ſervant,
J O H N   A N D R E,
Adjutant General.

(Addreſſed)
His Excellency
General Sir Henry Clinton, K. B.
&c. &c. &c.

Copy of a letter from His Excellency General Waſhington, to His Excellency Sir Henry Clinton.

Head Quarters, Sept. 30, 1780.
S I R,

IN anſwer to your Excellency's letter of the 26th inſtant, which I had the honour to receive, I am to inform you, that Major André was taken under ſuch circumſtances as would have juſtified the moſt ſummary proceedings againſt him. I determined, however, to refer his caſe to the examination and deciſion of a Board of General Officers, who have reported, on his free and voluntary confeſſion and letters,----" That he came on " ſhore from the Vulture ſloop of war in the night of " the twenty-firſt of September inſtant," &c. &c. as in the report of the Board of General Officers.

From theſe proceedings it is evident Major André was employed in the execution of meaſures very foreign to the objects of flags of truce, and ſuch as they were never meant to authoriſe or countenance in the moſt diſtant degree ; and this gentleman confeſſed, with the greateſt candor, in the courſe of his examination, " That it was "impoſſible for him to ſuppoſe he came on ſhore, under " the ſanction of a flag."

I have the honour to be your Excellency's
Moſt obedient and moſt humble ſervant,
G.   W A S H I N G T O N.

(Addreſſed)
His Excellency Sir Henry Clinton.

In this letter, Major André's of the 29th of September to Sir Henry Clinton, was tranſmitted.

New-York,

New-York, 29, Sept. 1780.

S I R,

PERSUADED that you are inclined rather to promote than prevent the civilities and acts of humanity, which the rules of war permit between civilized nations, I find no difficulty in reprefenting to you, that feveral letters and meffages fent from hence have been difregarded, are unanfwered, and the flags of truce that carried them, detained. As I ever have treated all flags of truce with civility and refpect, I have a right to hope, that you will order my complaint to be immediately redreffed.

Major André, who vifited an officer commanding in a diftrict at his own defire, and acted in every circumftance agreeable to his direction, I find is detained a prifoner; my friendfhip for him leads me to fear he may fuffer fome inconvenience for want of neceffaries; I wifh to be allowed to fend him a few, and fhall take it as a favour if you will be pleafed to permit his fervant to deliver them. In Sir Henry Clinton's abfence it becomes a part of my duty to make this reprefentation and requeft.

I am, Sir, your Excellency's
Moft obedient humble fervant,
JAMES ROBERTSON,
Lt. General.

His Excellency
General Wafhington.

Tappan, Sept. 30, 1780.

S I R,

I HAVE juft received your letter of the 29th. Any delay which may have attended your flags has proceeded from accident, and the peculiar circumftances of the occafion,---not from intentional neglect or violation. The letter that admitted of an anfwer, has received one as early as it could be given with propriety, tranfmitted by a flag this morning. As to meffages, I am uninformed of any that have been fent.

The neceffaries for Major André will be delivered to him, agreeable to your requeft.

I am, Sir,
Your moft obedient humble fervant,
G. WASHINGTON.

His Excellency
Lieut. General Robertfon,
New-York.

New-York,

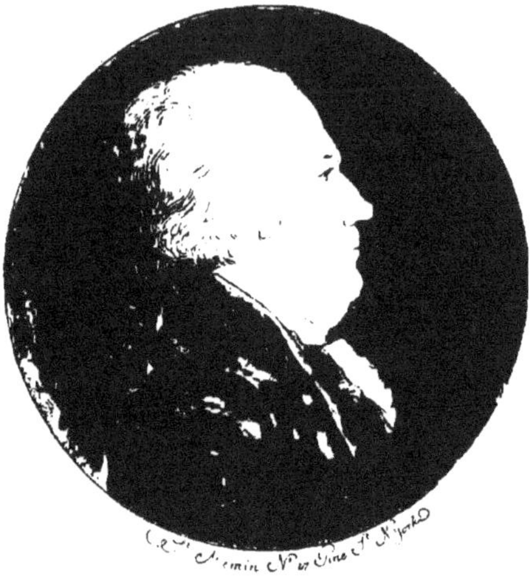

New-York, Sept. 30. 1780.

S I R,

FROM your Excellency's letter of this date, I am perfuaded the Board of General Officers, to whom you referred the cafe of Major Andrè, can't have been rightly informed of all the circumftances on which a judgment ought to be formed. I think it of the higheft moment to humanity, that your Excellency fhould be perfectly apprized of the ftate of this matter, before you proceed to put that judgment in execution.

For this reafon, I fhall fend His Excellency Lieut. General Robertfon, and two other gentlemen, to give you a true ftate of facts, and to declare to you my fentiments and refolutions. They will fet out to-morrow as early as the wind and tide will permit, and wait near Dobbs's ferry for your permiffion and fafe conduct, to meet your Excellency, or fuch perfons as you may appoint, to converfe with them on this fubject.

I have the honour to be, your Excellency's
Moft obedient and moft humble fervant,
H. CLINTON.

P. S. The Hon. Andrew Elliot, Efq. Lieut. Governor, and the Hon. William Smith, Chief Juftice of this province, will attend His Excellency Lieut. General Robertfon.

H. C.

His Excellency General Wafhington.

Lieut. General Robertfon, Mr. Elliot, and Mr. Smith came up in a flag veffel to Dobb's ferry, agreeable to the above letter. The two laft were not fuffered to land. General Robertfon was permitted to come on fhore, and was met by Major General Greene, who verbally reported that General Robertfon mentioned to him in fubftance what is contained in his letter of the 2d of October to General Wafhington.

New-York, Oct. 1, 1780.

S I R,

I TAKE this opportunity to inform your Excellency, that I confider myfelf no longer acting under the commiffion of Congrefs: Their laft to me being among my papers at Weft-point, you, Sir, will make fuch ufe of it, as you think proper.

C   At

At the same time, I beg leave to assure your Excellency, that my attachment to the true interest of my country is invariable, and that I am actuated by the SAME PRINCIPLE which has ever been the GOVERNING RULE of my conduct, in this unhappy contest.

I have the honour to be, very respectfully,
Your Excellency's most obedient humble servant,

B. ARNOLD.

His Excellency General Washington.

Greyhound Schooner, Flag of Truce,
Dobbs's Ferry, October 2, 1780.

S I R,

A NOTE I have from General Greene, leaves me in doubt if his memory had served him, to relate to you with exactness the substance of the conversation that had passed between him and myself, on the subject of Major Andrè. In an affair of so much consequence to my friend, to the two armies, and humanity, I would leave no possibility of a misunderstanding, and therefore take the liberty to put in writing the substance of what I said to General Greene.

I offered to prove, by the evidence of Colonel Robinson and the officers of the Vulture, that Major André went on shore at General Arnold's desire, in a boat sent for him with a flag of truce; that he not only came ashore with the knowledge and under the protection of the General who commanded in the district, but that he took no step while on shore but by direction of General Arnold, as will appear by the inclosed letter from him to your Excellency.

Under these circumstances I could not, and hoped you would not, consider Major André as a spy, for any improper phrase in his letter to you.

The facts he relates correspond with the evidence I offer; but he admits a conclusion that does not follow. The change of cloaths and name was ordered by General Arnold, under whose direction he necessarily was, while within his command. As General Greene and I did not agree in opinion, I wished, that disinterested gentlemen of knowledge of the law of war and nations, might be asked their opinion on the subject; and mentioned Monsieur Knyphausen, and General Rochambault.

I related that a Captain Robinson had been delivered to Sir Henry Clinton as a spy, and undoubtedly was such; but that it being signified to him that you were desirous

that

that this man fhould be exchanged, he had ordered him to be exchanged.

I wifhed that an intercourfe of fuch civilities, as the rules of war admit of, might take off many of its horrors. I admitted that Major André had a great fhare of Sir Henry Clinton's efteem, and that he would be infinitely obliged by his liberation ; and that if he was permitted to return with me, I would engage to have any perfon you would be pleafed to name fet at liberty.

I added, that Sir Henry Clinton had never put to death any perfon for a breach of the rules of war, though he had, and now has, many in his power. Under the prefent circumftances, much good may arife from humanity, much ill from the want of it. If that could give any weight, I beg leave to add, that your favourable treatment of Major André, will be a favour I fhould ever be intent to return to any you hold dear.

My memory does not retain with the exactnefs I could wifh, the words of the letter which General Greene fhewed me from Major André to your Excellency. For Sir Henry Clinton's fatisfaction, I beg you will order a copy of it to be fent to me at New-York.

I have the honour to be, your Excellency's
Moft obedient and moft humble fervant,
JAMES ROBERTSON.
His Excellency General Wafhington.

New-York, October 1, 1780.
S I R,

THE polite attention fhewn by your Excellency and the Gentlemen of your family to Mrs. Arnold, when in diftrefs, demand my grateful acknowledgment and thanks, which I beg leave to prefent.

From your Excellency's letter to Sir Henry Clinton, I find a Board of General Officers have given it as their opinion, that Major André comes under the defcription of a fpy : My good opinion of the candor and juftice of thofe Gentlemen leads me to believe, that if they had been made fully acquainted with every circumftance refpecting Major André, that they would by no means have confidered him in the light of a fpy, or even of a prifoner. In juftice to him, I think it my duty to declare, that he came from on board the Vulture at my particular requeft, by a flag fent on purpofe for him by Jofhua Smith, Éfq. who had permiffion to go to Dobbs's ferry to carry letters, and for other purpofes not mentioned,
and

and to return. This was done as a blind to the fpy boats: Mr. Smith at the same time had my private directions to go on board the Vulture, and bring on fhore Col. Robinfon, or Mr. John Anderfon, which was the name 1 had requefted Major André to affume : At the fame time 1 defired Mr. Smith to inform him, that he fhould have my protection, and a fafe paffport to return in the fame boat, as foon as our bufinefs was compleated. As feveral accidents intervened to prevent his being fent on board, 1 gave him my paffport to return by land. Major André came on fhore in his uniform (without difguife) which with much reluctance, at my particular and preffing inftance, he exchanged for another coat. 1 furnifhed him with a horfe and faddle, and pointed out the route by which he was to return. And as commanding officer in the department, 1 had an undoubted right to tranfact all thefe matters ; which, if wrong, Major André ought by no means to fuffer for them.

But if, after this juft and candid reprefentation of Major André's cafe, the Board of General Officers adhere to their former opinion, 1 fhall fuppofe it dictated by paffion and refentment ; and if that Gentleman fhould fuffer the feverity of their fentence, 1 fhall think myfelf bound by every tie of duty and honour, to retaliate on fuch unhappy perfons of your army, as may fall within my power, that the refpect due to flags, and to the law of nations, may be better underftood and obferved.

1 have further to obferve, that forty of the principal inhabitants of South-Carolina have juftly forfeited their lives, which have hitherto been fpared by the clemency of His Excellency Sir Henry Clinton, who cannot in juftice extend his mercy to them any longer, if Major André fuffers ; which in all probability will open a fcene of blood at which humanity will revolt

Suffer me to intreat your Excellency, for your own and the honour of humanity, and the love you have of juftice, that you fuffer not an unjuft fentence to touch the life of Major André.

But if this warning fhould be difregarded, and he fuffer, 1 call heaven and earth to witnefs, that your Excellency will be juftly anfwerable for the torrent of blood that may be fpilt in confequence.

I have the honour to be, with due refpect, your Excellency's
Moft obedient and very humble fervant,

B. ARNOLD.

His Excellency General Washington.

Tappan,

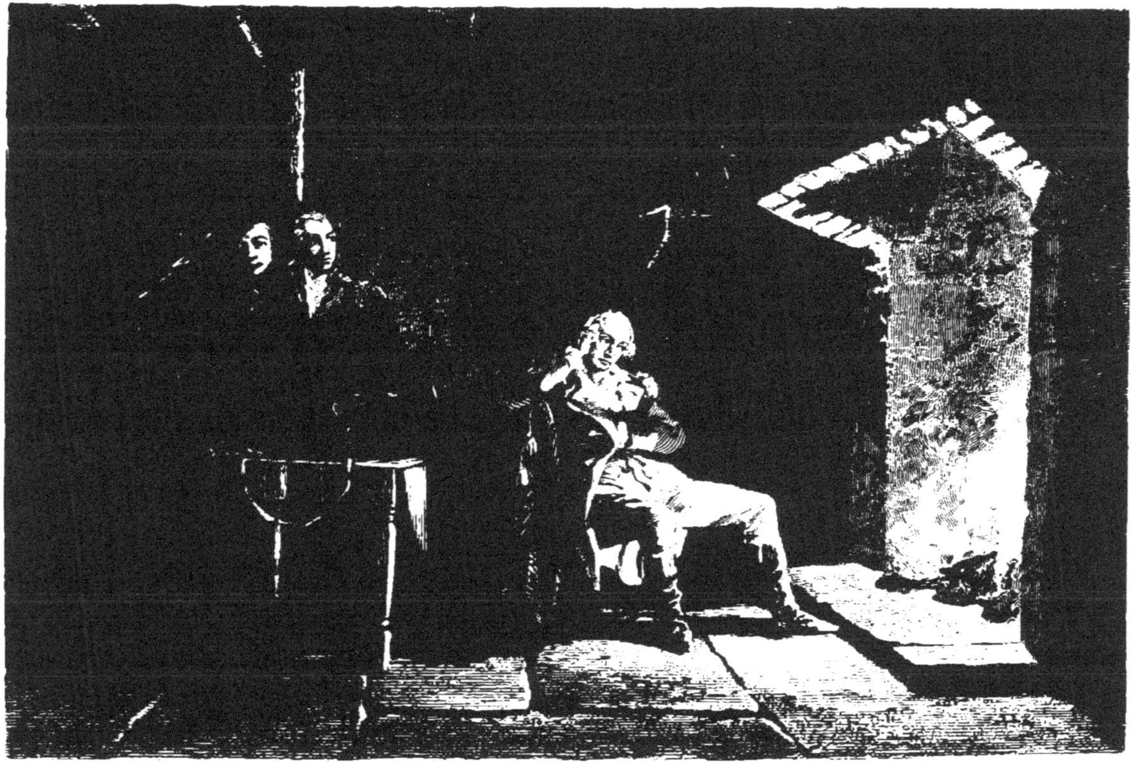

WASHINGTON [illegible]

21

Tappan, Oct. 1, 1780.

S I R,

BUOY'D above the terror of death, by the confcioufnefs of a life devoted to honourable purfuits, and ftained with no action that can give me remorfe, I truft that the requeft I make to your Excellency at this ferious period, and which is to foften my laft moments, will not be rejected.

Sympathy towards a foldier will furely induce your Excellency and a military tribunal to adopt the mode of my death to the feelings of a man of honour.

Let me hope, Sir, that if ought in my character impreffes you with efteem towards me, if ought in my misfortunes marks me as the victim of policy and not of refentment, I fhall experience the operation of thefe feelings in your breaft, by being informed that I am not to die on a gibbet.

I have the honour to be, your Excellency's
Moft obedient and moft humble fervant,
JOHN ANDRE,
Adj. Gen. to the Britifh army.

The time which elapfed between the capture of Major André, which was on the morning of the 23d of Sept. and his execution, which did not take place till 12 o'clock on the 3d of October;---the mode of trying him;---his letter to Sir Henry Clinton, K. B. on the 29th of September, in which he faid, " I receive the greateft attention from his " Excellency General Wafhington, and from every per- " fon under whofe charge I happen to be placed;"---not to mention many other acknowledgements which he made of the good treatment he received;---muft evince, that the proceedings againft him were not guided by paffion or refentment. The practice and ufage of war were againft his requeft, and made the indulgence he folicited, circumftanced as he was, inadmiffible.

Publifhed by order of Congrefs,

CHARLES THOMSON, *Secretary.*

www.ingramcontent.com/pod-product-compliance
Lightning Source LLC
Chambersburg PA
CBHW031816090426
42739CB00008B/1293